Jannis Kounellis

Jannis Kounellis

MODERN ART OXFORD

The Visual Poetics of Jannis Kounellis

Suzanne Cotter and Andrew Nairne

It is perhaps paradoxical that an artist as conscious of history as Jannis Kounellis should be so closely associated with one particular art movement; that of *Arte Povera*. However the radicality of his practice in the 1960s and 70s – transforming the space of the gallery with live horses or burning gas flames, exhibiting a parrot as a painting, or sitting at a table laden with fragments of antique sculpture while wearing a gold mask of Apollo – signalled not the culmination of his art but the beginning of a highly poetic visual language which he has continued to develop to the present.

For Kounellis, the gallery is a space in which the artist can act. It is a space of encounter which the artist invests with meaning. Kounellis's engagement with the social and historic context and with the material fabric of a given space is critical to his art. As well as creating installations in museums and galleries around the world, he has created remarkable interventions in Renaissance palaces, Jewish synagogues, Byzantine churches and old market places. He has also created dramatic installations in warehouses and in the holds of cargo boats. They are all places redolent with history, human endeavour; with the passage of people, of goods and of time.

For anyone first encountering the work of Kounellis today, it may come as a surprise to learn that this creator of intensely physical art works trained as a painter. Kounellis still describes himself as a painter and his works as paintings. He has developed the formal language of art making, and of painting in particular, to speak of larger concerns that operate in the realm of the real. His work translates the *chiaroscuro* and realism of Caravaggio, the expressive materiality of Van Gogh and the 'all over' technique of Pollock into a compelling visual and physical experience. The viewer occupies the same space as the composition. He translates the painterly relationship of figure to ground into the space of real situations. The twelve horses tethered around the gallery wall (1969) not only alludes to a tradition of equestrian statuary, it is a majestic composition that lives, breathes and smells. As an artist who emerged out of the political ferment of the 1960's, Kounellis has developed this relationship between figure and ground into a relationship between the fragment and the whole; that is, of the individual to society and of society to history. As he has stated: "There is no evolution in art independent of the events which govern it. In order to given an account of the development of an artist's work, one can't talk exclusively about the work itself without linking it to the significant encounters he has had, to his particular human experiences as well as to social and historical events which are more vast and far-reaching."[1]

Born in 1936 in Piraeus, the busy port of Athens, Kounellis has lived since the age of twenty in Rome. But the sights, sounds, sensations and drama of a port have never left him: piles of coal, the smell of tar, sacks of potatoes and grains; trains, boats and people constantly arriving and departing. Acknowledging the power of memory and lived experience, his work developed out of the contradictions and tensions of the post war era. It's huge ambition is the constant search for synthesis and the potential resolution of these contradictions through a carefully balanced harmony.

At Modern Art Oxford, Kounellis has addressed the varying scaled spaces of the Gallery's architecture to create a harmonious whole. Exploiting the riveted metal columns, the vaulted iron ceilings and the brick walls of the building's original Victorian architecture with the placement of his works, he has unified the disparate and enhanced those elements which, in the aesthetic domain of the art space, usually remain unobserved. At the same time, each space plays a carefully orchestrated role in a more dramatic and highly poetic narrative.

In the first space of the exhibition, seven large steel panels are propped up on old wooden chairs arranged against the walls. Small pieces of coal have been sewn onto the surface with wire. The irregular shapes and absorbent blackness of the coal is arranged across each panel in varying lines, like so many calculations on an abacus. The work speaks of calculated measure and of randomness, of language and of economics. Kounellis has conceived of the exhibition around two of the gallery's largest spaces and around two contrasting yet inextricably related bodies of work: one connected to the earliest enunciations of his burgeoning artistic language; the other, a new installation created specifically for Oxford. In the case of the earlier work, Kounellis has staged what he describes as "a hypothetical retrospective". Raised up on a platform of wooden market tables are some of his earliest works, made when he was still a student at the Accademia di Belle Arti in Rome, together with pieces that have long ago entered into the canonical lexicon of what we know as *Arte Povera*: the burlap sacks filled with grains and coal; the aromatic mounds of ground coffee on suspended metal scales; the metal relief in the form of a daisy that, before the safety regulations of more recent times, would hiss jets of blue gas flame. Kounellis has composed an extraordinary tableau, like a seventeenth century Still Life in which each exquisitely rendered element carries multiple meanings and messages. The largely sepia tones of the earlier works are highlighted by the vivid colours of an aquarium and two gold fish swimming in a white china bowl in which Kounellis has also placed the silver blade of a black handled knife. Originally created as an image for one of his exhibition posters, this second work confronts the viewer with two antithetical realities. If Kounellis's composition here moves us in his staging of his own past, the framing of these iconic – and hence valuable – works subtly suggests the art with which his relationship has often been uneasy. More significantly, this presentation reiterates Kounellis's insistence that none of his works made in the present can be separated from those made in the past and that all of his work oscillates between these two states.

His new installation, created for the Upper Gallery at Modern Art Oxford, is a *tour de force* of sculptural eloquence. Unfolding like the lines of a Futurist painting, a latticework of iron beams marches across the volume of the gallery space. Countering its menacing crystalline perspective is a multicoloured floor of woven Turkish rugs which seem to hold the metallic force of the structure in silent suspension. A black hat and coat – a leitmotif in the artist's work since the mid-seventies – hangs off one of the beams at the far end. As with all of Kounellis's work, the tension between hard and soft, between force and resistance is ever present. The formation of three iron beams making up each of the overlapping elements, which Kounellis has used in a number of major installations in recent years, refers to the falling cross from Christ's passion – a powerful symbol of Western iconography. The riveted iron speaks of railway sidings, of an industrial age, of battle lines, grinding noise, speed and destruction. The carpets speak of a more intimate human-ity; of story telling, of exchange, of comfort and of warmth. Kounellis describes this work as "a clash of civilisations; a meeting of technology and spirituality". Sculpturally, it is an extraordinary work, conceived with the economy of an artist at the height of his powers, and expressed with a poetry that is impossible to ignore.

We are hugely grateful to Jannis Kounellis for accepting our invitation to present his work at Modern Art Oxford and for the inspiration and generosity he has brought to this task.

It is his first solo exhibition in a public gallery in Britain since his installation for the Henry Moore Foundation's studios at Dean Clough in Halifax in 1993. The exhibition would not have been possible without the collaboration of Michelle Coudray, to whom we extend our deepest thanks. Our sincerest thanks also to those collectors who generously supported the exhibition with the loan of important works.

We are indebted to those Friends and Patrons who have supported the exhibition, and to the Italian Cultural Institute, London, The Henry Moore Foundation, the Stanley Thomas Johnson Foundation, the Estate of Tom Bendhem, and Illycaffé for their support, without which the exhibition and this publication would not have been possible.

In producing the exhibition and the publication, we have had to rely on the assistance and expertise of many people. We would especially like to thank Kounellis's assistants Damiano Urbani, Vangjel Caci and Joel Anitori; Elisabetta Campolongo at the artist's studio in Rome, and Manolis Baboussis for his wonderful work on the installation photography. Herman Lelie, with Stefania Bonelli, has designed this beautiful publication with great sensitivity; we thank both of them. Lastly, but not least, we would like thank our colleagues at Modern Art Oxford who have worked with energy and skill to make this exhibition possible, in particular: Miria Swain, Dawn Scarfe, Tom Legg and his installation crew Matt Golden, Adam J. Maynard, Ruairiadh O'Connell, Louise Taylor, Ross Taylor, Stuart Turner and Mia Young.

1
'Structure and Sensibility', Interview with Willoughby Sharp, 1972, in M. Codognato, M. d'Argenzio (eds.), *Echoes in the Darkness. Jannis Kounellis: Writings and Interviews*, Trolley, London, 2003, p.147

Untitled 1967

Untitled 1969

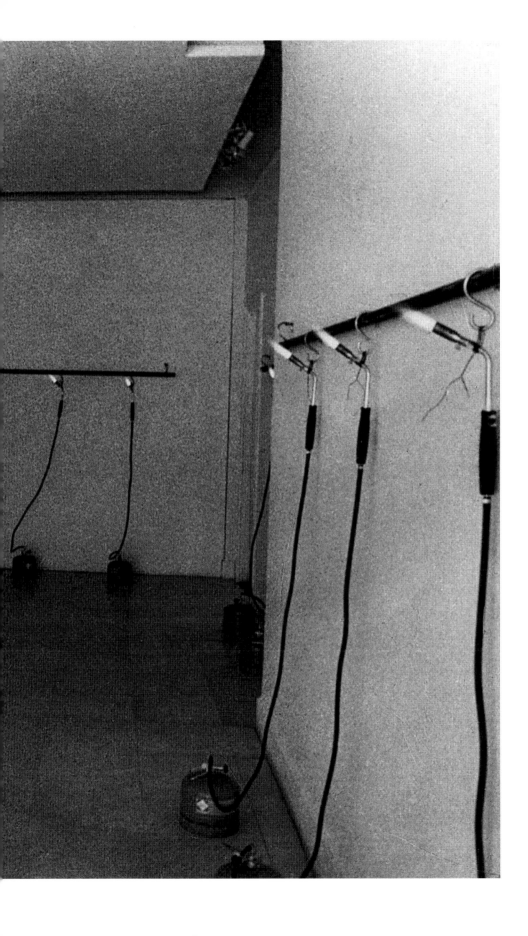

top: *Untitled* 1969   bottom: *Untitled* 1967

Untitled 1967

Untitled 1969

An Engaged Modern Painter

Adachiara Zevi

Redefining the terrain

Doubt, Art and Civil Passion is the title of an article published by Jannis Kounellis in the culturally, politically and socially committed journal *MicroMega*: an opportunity to formulate the ideas underpinning over forty years of work. In this article, Kounellis writes: "Globalisation is like a lake with shores that present no barrier. You think that countries no longer exist and that the dream of eliminating any differences that even remotely recall conflict has finally come true."[1] This trend is evident in the history of the relationship between Arte Povera, of which Kounellis was a key protagonist, and its adversary, the Transavanguardia.[2] Ideological allegiances, differences and dialectical clashes become reconciled, even out and fade away with the passing of time and the distancing of events, reducing cultural debate to the shabby pursuit of consensus.

If it is to acquire plausibility, a revision and rewriting of this history is needed. This is exactly what has happened and is happening as regards both Arte Povera and the Transavanguardia. In the more general historical and political sphere, it is also what has long been pointed out by a handful of scholars of courage and integrity like Sergio Luzzatto, whose recently published work *La crisi dell'antifascismo* sounds a warning against the efforts to undermine the antifascist foundations of the Italian Republic born out of the Resistance. "Fascism and antifascism are receding into the past. The new generations are less and less involved in that clash of values. But the future is born out of history, not the deletion of the past. A mature country can and perhaps must come to terms with a divided memory."[3] This revisionism in both the historical and the art-historical spheres affects Jannis Kounellis personally, given his conviction that "the history of art cannot be separated from the history of society".[4] A longstanding antifascist and left-wing militant, he was a leading figure in Arte Povera and an opponent of the return to order exemplified by the Transavanguardia right from its birth in the mid-1970s.

With the sole exception of *The Knot: Arte Povera at P.S1* (New York, 1985), Arte Povera has been given little consideration outside of Europe. When *Zero to Infinity: Arte Povera 1962–72*, first shown at Tate Modern in 2001, was presented at the Walker Art Center in Minneapolis and other museums across the United States, the movement's historical mentor Germano Celant was absent and its artists marginalised. The Anglo-American exhibition mummified what was by definition vital, dynamic and precarious, and the history outlined in the catalogue was distorted to fit in with preconceived critical theses. The essays played down the movement's revolutionary significance and identified its particularities as provincial in relation to the prevailing American art of the time. A clear example is provided by Robert Lumley's text, 'Spaces of Arte Povera', where the untranslatable nature of the term "arte povera" was taken as proof of confinement to a particularly Italian context and the group's identity characterised more by what it opposed, namely Minimalism and Pop Art, than by what the individual approaches of the artists shared.[5] Lumley points out that Arte Povera was largely unknown outside Italy until 1968 and that when the Italian artists arrived on the international stage, with the exhibitions *Prospect '68*, *Nine at Castelli* (1969) and *When Attitudes Become Form* (1969), exhibiting their work side by side with the Americans, the scenario had changed completely. Borders had disappeared and with them every form of national belonging: "The attempt to make Arte Povera a transnational category had failed. Unlike Conceptual Art and Land Art (…) Arte Povera slipped into relative obscurity. Moreover, it was debased metaphorically when in non-Italian usage it was made to signify merely an attitude toward materials (…). Arte Povera did not have its Marinetti. It was not a movement. Arte Povera's development within city-based art scenes was empirical but not ideological, experimental but not politically oriented."[6] It is worth discussing two points raised in Lumley's text: namely the confusion between identity and nationalism, and the relationship between Arte Povera and the contemporary movements of Pop Art and Minimalism.

Kounellis sees Arte Povera as a generation more than a movement. It was born in a precise historical context, namely the post-war period of a defeated country bereft of civilization, values and identity. It was the task of art, like literature, poetry and cinema, "to tell the tale of the enormous drama of loss", not with resignation but rather with a drive to rebuild the lost integrity and totality. "I seek the scattered history in fragments, both emotional and formal. I seek unity in a dramatic way though difficult to grasp, though utopian, though impossible and hence dramatic. […] I will not succeed in putting the totality back together, but the honest endeavour of a painter is to try, not to give up on the difficulties history presents you with, to embark on this extremely long journey."[7] To invent a language capable of communicating simultaneously the sense of loss and the striving for totality, a condition and a goal, this was the challenge for Kounellis and his generation.

On arriving in Rome from Greece in 1956, Kounellis looked around for points of reference but found little that struck him as plausible. Not realism, which records reality without judging or criticising it; not abstract art, which suppresses it; not the compromise of Neo-Cubism; not *Art Informel*, which transfers the problem to the expression of individual malaise. At its peak in the mid-50s, *Art Informel* had already exhausted all its propulsive thrust and Kounellis shared the desire to move past it: "The problem is to understand what has driven us to leave painting behind. My first dialectic moment was with Informalism, but not because I was an Informalist. I lived through the tail-end of it and I tried to get out. That's how I realised the substance of Pollock and the flimsiness of Fautrier. Fautrier's centralizing schema struck me as phantasmagoric. It wasn't real. Pollock had instead tried to destroy centrality. My generation emerged from this realisation, or rather, I did. The opening was neither scenic nor spectacular. The goal was to find a reality of the image, which centrality did not possess."[8] There are two key ideas here: to destroy the centrality of the painting and to find the reality of the image.

In spite of his supposed provincialism, Kounellis's initial point of reference is the master of American action painting, Jackson Pollock. For Kounellis, Pollock's dripping technique expressed the search for a new identity through a revolution in language. Rather than force the space of reality into the reduced space of the painting, it opened up the space of painting to reality. Other possible references for Kounellis were the combine paintings of Robert Rauschenberg, who had exhibited his works at the Galleria La Tartaruga in Rome in 1959, the year before Kounellis had his first exhibition there. Another was Jasper Johns, whose "flag" proclaimed the identity of the painting and the real object. Kounellis's problem was, however, neither contaminating the painting with reality nor establishing an identity between reality and representation, but rather replacing the representation of reality with the presentation of the same. This is demonstrated by the difference between the sequence of letters and numbers forced by Johns into a square grid and the letters, numbers and arrows marking the great white sheets Kounellis exhibited in 1960 at La Tartaruga. Fragmentary, displaced, turned upside-down, they escape from the support to arrive in space like the stuttering of a new language yet to become a whole. Their random character, however, is only apparent. The letters are all the same size and impersonally painted. Both abstract and spatially undefined, they translate the introverted space of Pollock's dripping into the public space of urban signage. In the same way, Kounellis played the part of Hugo Ball in the Cabaret Voltaire when he dressed up in those same sheets and sang the letters in the gallery.

What Kounellis was telling us is that no creation is possible without an awareness of the past. At the same time, history cannot repeat itself slavishly if it is to have present-day relevance. It must be disguised and discreetly worked into the image, like a decontextualized fragment, so as to give it substance and credibility. Hence his assertion: "I believe that if a work of art is to exist as such, it must be born out of a historical necessity, live through a historical situation, and establish itself as indispensable language at that time." It is significant that today, faced with the globalized boom of "kilometric museums masterfully designed and destined to receive a million visitors a year", more interested in exhibiting motorcycles and fashion parades than works of art, Kounellis once again invokes the Dadaist model of the Cabaret Voltaire.

In metabolising Pollock's dripping into the centrifugal arrangement of letters, Kounellis translated a formal solution into a methodological principle in which the limited vocabulary of letters would give way to the extraordinary richness of a lexicon of the real. The oblique arrangement of letters stencilled on coal sacks and sheet metal is echoed in the rows of flames along the walls of the Gallery Iolas in Paris in 1969 and in the iron girders used over the years with coal sacks, reams of paper, rolled sheets of lead, overcoats or painted pages. Presented in Oxford in their original version, the letter paintings are among the many fragments on the stage of Kounellis's history – a humble platform made up of an assortment of ordinary tables recalling his *Untitled* of 1973, when the artist, his face covered by a mask of Apollo, sat at a table strewn with fragments of sculpture.

While the letters yearned for the free dimension of space, two works of 1966 announced their accomplished liberation. One featured a white surface bearing three white roses made of fabric inside a series of cages containing live birds. If by definition the frame delimits and defends the painting from the exterior, the exterior forces its way into the painting here, animating it and forcing its owner to take loving care of it every day, as was soon to happen with works featuring a parrot, horses and sides of beef. Cages also became part of Kounellis's armoury from this time on: hanging from iron girders, re-populating the remains of the ancient Synagogue at Ostia in 2002 and standing empty on the shelves of the old library in the church of San Augustín in Mexico City in 1999. Moreover, the *Untitled* of 1966 "is born out of a historical situation and establishes itself as indispensable language" at that time. Minimalism was consecrated in the same year with the exhibition *Primary Structures* at the Jewish Museum in New York. While suggestive of the modular structures of Minimalism in terms of form and material, Kounellis's identical cages of iron set at regular distances and inhabited by living beings actually challenge their inertia and self-referentiality, just as the hand-painted, topsy-turvy letters challenge those of Roy Lichtenstein, simply transferred from the sphere of advertising to that of art. The work also reinterprets the structure of the medieval icon with its central and hieratic figure of the Madonna surrounded by saints engaged in their everyday occupations.

Caught between consumeristic icon and serialized containment, the polysemy of Kounellis's work thus points to the winding and dramatic path of a post-war European identity. As Kounellis explains, "When you talk about Italian painting, you talk about a possible diversity with respect to the iron-clad logic of the square. Our work has thrown the square into crisis along with its apologetic and a priori character. There are two possibilities: either to have a unique image or to represent a cultural situation. The unique definition is idealist, linked to the puritan and Calvinist world." [9] Unlike Mondrian's and even Malevich's square, the minimalist square translated "the idea of history" into a "strictly metrical fact"; in other words, it countered composition with repetition. As with the diagonal flight of letters, the contrast between the rigidity of the cages and the vitality of the birds, between the two-dimensionality of the support and the three-dimensionality of the subject, becomes poetic and method-ological substance to indicate a dialectic between opposing positions: background and figure, container and content, structural and organic, tough and fragile, hard and soft, held and hanging. Given Kounellis's warning that the history of art is inseparable from the history of society, the stakes are much higher. The contest is between "form as power", that is, geometric therefore symmetrical, and "form as opposition", that is uncertain, erratic and asymmetrical; between apologetics and criticism, assent and dissent.

A second work by Kounellis of 1966 transfers the same dialectic from the surface to space by taking the entire architectural container, in this case the artist's studio, as a support. A great curtain of burlap sacks pinned to the wall slumps to the ground under the force of gravity. One hundred kilos of coal lies alongside in a corner. The comparison with fresco is very apt: "The dimension is the architectural support. The formation of an image takes place inside architectural borders. One hundred kilos of coal in a room has the physical dimensions of a fresco." If the modular structures confine themselves to echoing the neutral cube of the gallery and the grid plan of the American metropolis, in a dimension midway between object and architecture, Kounellis addresses the exhibition space right from this very first text as "a dramatic, theatrical cavity in which to act", working with it and against it. The difference between Europe and America, between a victorious country and a defeated one, between one possessed of absolute truths and certainties and one struggling desperately to endow its ruins with image and dignity, cannot therefore be reduced to the simple difference in materials. It is far greater and regards two diametrically opposite artistic and political visions. As Kounellis insists in *MicroMega*, "The identity of modern Europe draws sustenance from diversity. Europeans do not have the monumental certainty of Americans, being in any case made critical by the depth of the tragedies they have lived through. This is what being European means: cultivating doubt and distance, and therefore adopting a critical stance." [10]

The heap of coal and the curtain of sacks confirm the accomplished disintegration of the painting into its constituent elements: the support and the image. The next step is the search for a new compositional order replacing the centrality of the painting but endowing it with equal credibility. "Once the centralizing idea of figuration has been destroyed, there are many others. There is a path of figurations. But all this must be meaningful and this chaos must be led toward a different order." [11] Kounellis started out on this path in 1967 in his exhibition at the Galleria L'Attico in Rome and in the exhibition inaugurating Arte Povera at La Bertesca in Genoa, indiscriminately incorporating the wall, the space and the architectural structure itself. A parrot is perched on a sheet of iron against a wall; *Untitled (Margherita di fuoco)* 1967 stands erect in space spitting fire; *Untitled (Carboniera)* 1967 is a rigid iron container full of coal, like *Untitled (Cotoniera)* 1967, overflowing with cotton wool, and other recipients full of earth and cactus, their size varying in relation to the weight of the material and the measurements of the room.

When Kounellis states that the letters have the same value as the parrot, he is alerting us to a crucial point: painting and the painting are not synonymous. It is possible to be a painter in space, using materials other than paintbrushes and canvas, because the problem of painting is creating images, constantly renewing the dialectic between figure and background regardless of method and technique. From cave paintings to medieval frescoes, from Renaissance perspective through Baroque theatricality all the way to the disintegration of Cubism, the dripping of Jackson Pollock, and the slashed canvas of Lucio Fontana, the history of art is the history of the meeting and clashing of these two poles. It is no coincidence that the approaches which eliminate this – from the hieratic Byzantine vision to monochromes, serialism and virtual art – declare themselves against or "beyond" painting. While the "Byzantine mentality obstructed the Renaissance era" in Greek culture, and American culture makes up for lack of history with unrestrained vitality, it is the "centrality of a humanist text" that must be asserted in Italy. In what sense? Does perspective place mankind at the centre of an infinite, continuous and homogenous space, deceiving painters that it faithfully reflects reality? In Kounellis's updating of perspective, the illusion of representation becomes the reality of presentation; spatial unity, the aggregation and stratification of heterogeneous, fragmentary and discontinuous elements; instead of receding the composition projects towards the viewer; the metaphor of the vanishing point, the human scale of the double bed, the door or the sheet of Fabriano paper. While Kounellis counters the choices offered by the painting as support – with only two exceptions – by limiting his supports to a specific size, he indulges himself with the 'figure'. The iron containers can hold scrap metal instead of cacti, books instead of cotton. The sheet metal can support sides of beef, coal sacks, flames chasing one another, shelves, oil lamps, pieces of wood, clothes, and dozens of other possibilities. Finding the gesture that unifies the fragment, the ideology that admits pluralism, this is the task Kounellis presents himself with. He is an engaged contemporary painter, whose points of reference are the "ideological painters like Masaccio or Caravaggio, people who put their name to their poetic opinions and defend them", whose paintings do not possess the medieval dogmatism of icons. His awareness of and insistence on the difference between Europe and America does not mean nationalistic protectionism. With regard to the exhibitions hosted between 1969 and 1971 in European *Kunstmuseums* and *Kunsthalles*, Kounellis asserts: "It is necessary to resume the discourse eliminating the borders and bring into play these multiple identities anchored to values, with a desire to understand the other," [12] And in the same article: "I recall our exhibitions of the 1960s, formalised outside the canvas and frame, which not only revolutionised the visual aspect but also undermined the foundations of a certain type of form that had come to represent conformity. They also offered a different hierarchy of values." [13]

Returning to *Zero to Infinity* and leaving aside the other contributions, we must draw attention to the text 'Now we begin' by Francesco Bonami, an Italian critic employed for many years in American museums and Director of the 2003 Venice Biennale. He claims that "the legacy of Renaissance philosophy overshadowed the autonomy of artistic production" and that Arte Povera, like all the other Italian artistic movements, is incapable of freeing itself from the legacy of the Renaissance, which "clouds its autonomy [...]. They have increased the number of materials but the relationship established with a handful of coal or a head of lettuce differs little essentially from that established by previous artists with a piece of marble." [14] Referring to Fellini's 1953 film, Bonami labels the arte povera artists as "*vitelloni*" (loafers), in their efforts to get away from the "parochialism of their origins while remaining attracted by the comforts of their historical and national identity". [15] Bonami draws this distinction between Arte Povera and Minimalism: "It is not an iconoclastic movement like Minimalism, even though both represent a sort of Lutheran reform that disrupts the existing aesthetic order, Arte Povera with a more organic approach and Minimalism along more abstract and theoretical lines", to the point that no member of the Arte Povera movement, not even Fabro, the most theoretical of the group, has ever produced theoretical and critical contributions of the same quality as Donald Judd! What the curators of the exhibition and the editors of the catalogue seem to pass over however, is the political and ideological opposition of that generation, something that reaction then suppression and now globalised standardisation have all endeavoured to exorcise. Bonami again: "Italy fell into oblivion between 1972 and 1978. The individual ability to propose changes was delegated to the collective dictatorship of the student movement, the trade unions and the terrorism of the Red Brigades, a phenomenon more real and tragic than the one described by Celant in his seminal article *Arte Povera: Notes for a guerrilla warfare*." [16]

In making the same mistake as the post-antifascist revisionists, i.e. exorcising antifascism by smearing it as terrorism, Bonami dismisses the opposition that shook the world in the 1970s, in which the artists of Arte Povera played an active and leading part, as a kind of terrorism. Fortunately, he continues, the saviours of the Transavanguardia, the "first generation to escape from the political miasma of the 1970s", then arrived on the scene. He not only dismisses as irrelevant the all-out opposition between Arte Povera and Transavanguardia but also claims that when Celant attempted in 1984–85 to reawaken the "long slumbering spirit" of Arte Povera, what the exhibitions "ironically reveal is that the artists had been affected by the explosion of Transavanguardia". From Kounellis to Pier Paolo Calzolari and Mario Merz, they had all succumbed to the seduction of painting, "now crucial for success on the international scene", Nor does it stop there. "Rather than invoke the legacy of Duchamp, Judd, Manzoni or Smithson, they take Goya, Latour, Cézanne, Kandinsky, Pollock and even Caravaggio as their points of reference, thus suggesting that painting is the skeleton in the cupboard throughout the trajectory of the post-war avant-garde movements like Arte Povera." Finally, Bonami suggests that the heirs, headed by their honorary graduate Maurizio Cattelan, are some sort of globalised hybrids that reject both the radical political stance of Arte Povera and the regressive pictorial aspirations of the Transavanguardia. But when did the collective and revolutionary trajectory of Arte Povera come to an end? For Bonami, it is in 1977, the year of the famous photograph of a crouched terrorist in a balaclava taking aim on a street in Milan in the "years of lead" which he chose as the cover illustration to his contribution, underscoring, once again, the equation: opposition equals terrorism.

Bonami's voice is by no means isolated. It is part of an international attitude towards the history of post-war Italy; to distort and disparage its originality and to silence the heretical voice of its leading figures, aided and abetted by its adversary the Transavanguardia, the subject of a large-scale exhibition in the splendid museum of Castello di Rivoli in 2003. In historicizing the phenomenon underpinning the postmodernism of the 1980s, its boundaries are blurred and its outlines and identity made hazy, stressing the aspects of continuity rather than discontinuity with respect to the previous art. As Ida Giannelli, the director of the museum, prudently opines, "The Transavanguardia and Neo-Expressionism have been seen, above all by American critics with sociological leanings like Benjamin Buchloh, as spearheads of a return to order to be combated as the expression of a reactionary culture. It is, however, difficult to agree with these views. The Transavanguardia did of course reverse certain salient features that have been typical of all modern culture. Theirs was, however, not a reaction against the avant-garde and their search for something new but rather a refusal to fetishize and ideologize the new elements. [...] No return to order, if this term is given an ideological value, but a meditated and non-canonical revaluation of the traditional tools."[17] In the same publication, Carolyn Christov-Bakargiev, the editor of an anthology on Arte Povera adds: "What would happen if we viewed the art of the Transavanguardia as a continuation and development of premises contained in the previous modern art rather than a transformation and radical break both with the art of the 1960s and with the art of Modernism?" Her conclusion is: "Despite all the postmodernist theories published between the 1960s and the 1980s, it could in fact be argued that Postmodernism does not exist at all as a separate cultural period. As time goes by, it looks more and more like a particular form of Modernism, not all of which was in fact rationalistic [...]. Alongside Paul Cézanne, Piet Mondrian and the Bauhaus movement, it also included Matisse, Van Gogh, Pablo Picasso and Marcel Duchamp as well as the Metaphysical painters De Chirico and Carrà in Italy."[18]

This thesis not only misrepresents the artists' poetic intentions but confuses an awareness of the deep and tragic sense of history with the idea of history as something that can be pillaged. It also fails to acknowledge that the Transavanguardia's lack of objectives, ideals and moral sense is the antithesis of modernity. If a prestigious institution like the Castello di Rivoli and those that followed its lead – the Pecci Museum in Prato with an exhibition on Paladino, Castello di Gennazzano with Cucchi, the Archaeological Museum of Naples with Clemente, and the Rome Museum of Contemporary Art with De Maria – all agree to undertake a revivalist operation of such scale, the stakes are unquestionably very high indeed. The goal seems to be to deny the subversive and revolutionary dialectic of an entire generation and lead it back into the mainstream of tradition, conformism, respectability and apologetics. And the most incredible thing is that the operation is endorsed even by people who lived through and were involved in the whole story, such as Germano Celant, whose review of the Rivoli exhibition in the magazine *L'Espresso* lumps Alberto Burri, Kounellis, Enzo Cucchi, Clemente and Mimmo Paladino together on the grounds of interaction between painting and materials "enriched by a private and enigmatic density that makes the active dimension of life felt with respect to the impersonal idea and the social project".[19]

Kounellis is an implacable opponent of all pacification: "In this particularly difficult political and hence cultural and artistic period, at a time when the official critics have adopted the theses of the restoration party and, without a doubt, will soon paint our work in the colours of the 20th century, I would like to draw your attention once again to the sensibility and internationalist, critical, imaginative, visionary and poetic problems of my generation."[20] These words were spoken on the occasion of the Pascali Prize in Bari in 1979, the very year in which Achille Bonito Oliva announced the birth of the Transavanguardia in *Flash Art*. The two positions are clearly irreconcilable. Bonito Oliva regards the "ideologism of Arte Povera and the tautology of Conceptual Art" as superseded in the name of a "primacy of art and the fragrance of the work that rediscovers delight in being exhibited, in its own richness, and in the material of painting no longer debased by ideological commitments and purely intellectual agitation".[21]

Kounellis's reply is that the problem is not painting but what is proposed: "It is not a question of dividing the world into those who paint and those who don't. It is necessary to see what you do, what images you have, what you propose. There is no painting without problems." He refers to *Les Demoiselles d'Avignon*, "what must always be thought of as purpose and imaginative opening, authentic invention in formal and also basic terms. All the rest is ridiculous."[22] And yet Bonami claims that in 1984–85, when Celant reunited the Arte Povera group for the exhibition *Coerenza incoerenza dall'arte povera al 1984* (Mole Antonelliana, Turin), the artists had all espoused the Transavanguardia cause. The article written by Celant for the catalogue proves the opposite. Not only does Celant describe the exhibition as an attempt to combat the return to order of the 1980s, he also addresses the "gesticulating theorists and masters of stylistic and citationist painting", and hurls thunderbolts against the "pomp and pageantry of stereotyped formulas", against painting that is a "hotchpotch of things already seen and read, where the enumeration of sources counts for more than triggering the angst of history" The twelve artists exhibited in Turin, including Kounellis, were meant to offer an unsettled, agitated, fragmentary, discontinuous and multifaceted iconoclastic viewpoint in opposition to an art moving within the reassuring boundaries of the "sacred icons": "The serenity of a calm and dull world that swallows up and eliminates all drama is challenged by an ever-changing plan of action of unknown and uncertain outcome [...], proceeding in terms of rifts and upheavals, revolutions and schisms of a constantly awkward nature that challenge the legitimisation of a monistic cult of art."[23]

It is an idea that is borne out by Kounellis's works as portending imminent disaster. A stuffed crow is perched on the fragments scattered over the table of the above-mentioned *Untitled* of 1973. Two more lie as if shot down in the vicinity of a city outline drawn on a wall. Bandages over the eyes of plaster casts allude to critical blindness and the bright flame of *Margherita di fuoco* is extinguished in the black smoke pouring out of chimneys. Nor did it end here. It was in Bari in 1979 that Kounellis first confronted the ancient works in the city's picture gallery with his own in a relationship of simple juxtaposition. *Carboniera* and *Margherita di fuoco*, small scales with coffee and the head of a classical statue, bandaged or with fire coming out of one ear, coexisted with paintings produced in the fourteenth and fifteenth centuries, the fertile period in which the Middle Ages slid towards the Renaissance. After other experiments – at the Stedelijk Van Abbemuseum in Eindhoven in 1981 and the Museo Capodimonte in Naples 1989 – it was not until 1999, in the church of San Carlo in Spoleto, that Kounellis conceived a work specifically for a chapel occupied by a seventeenth century deposition: four iron girders like elongated limbs compressing a fifth and larger element wrapped in a long white shroud. Equally dramatic, Kounellis's "painting" historically recalls but linguistically breaks away from the one above it. For the exhibition *Incontri* at the Galleria Borghese, Rome, in 2003, which involved seven contemporary artists and seven of the gallery's works, Kounellis addressed Caravaggio's *David and Goliath* with a wooden cross thrust into a circle of coal sacks. And in Florence, invited together with four other artists to respond to Michelangelo's *David* in the Accademia on the occasion of its fifth centenary, Kounellis ignored the guest of honour and, instead, constructed a labyrinth around the two *Prisoners* housed in the same gallery; unfinished, writhing works of roughly-hewn stone. The labyrinth reveals a part of Kounellis's history to the elevated gaze of one of the *Prisoners*, namely a heap of coal in a corner, and another part to the other statue and the viewer, a huge dense, solid black stain painted on a white sheet and held down by an iron girder, albeit filtered through an iron grill.

A Pioneer of Space
As pointed out, the great conquest of Kounellis's generation was to break away from painting, leaving the studio "with hands in pockets", and to conceive the work in relation to place. In addressing every new challenge, Kounellis does not confine himself to studying plans and cross sections but moves quickly all over the space so as to capture its spirit, to penetrate its history, context and traditions, and involve them in his "one-act plays". More than others, ever since 1969, when he inaugurated the garage of the Galleria L'Attico with twelve live horses arranged around its

perimeter, Kounellis has played a pioneering role, addressing every type of space: canonical and anomalous, elevated and humble, anonymous and architecturally characterised, secular and religious, private and public, indoor and outdoor. To name but a few, he inaugurated the Espai Poblenou Foundation in Barcelona in 1990, exhibiting sides of beef for the first time, the Pulheim Synagogue the following year, the Galleria Salara in Bologna in 1995, and the imposing Museum Ludwig in der Halle Kalk, an old glass-cutting factory near Cologne, two years later. His declaration that the "horse had the same relationship with the gallery as the parrot with the structure" confirms the dialectic between a rigid and inert background and a dynamic, living "figure". It was again in 1969, walling up a doorway in the town of San Benedetto del Tronto with stones, that he worked for the first time directly on the architectural structure, constructing an image precisely to those measurements, exactly the same as the heap of coal in the corner. If the system is ancient, in use in Greece and Southern Italy, the free and irregular pattern of stones again clashes with Minimalist modularity. Compare Sol LeWitt's structures of standard concrete bricks. The dialectic between structure and sensibility takes shape in the contrast between the smooth wall of the gallery and the rough wall of stones.

As with the letters, the sheet metal and the containers, the solutions are enriched and multiply over time in the continuity of method: at the Belvedere in Prague, the Martin Gropius-Bau in Berlin, the Wiener Secession & Am Steinhof in Vienna, and the Art Museum of the Helsinki Atheneum, the stones being replaced with folded sacks, wooden sleepers, plaster casts and bells. And above all books, as in the harrowing installation in the National Library of Sarajevo, where two million books went up in smoke during the siege. Kounellis crammed the twelve openings of the ambulatory giving onto the central hexagonal hall with different materials all picked up on the spot to construct a unified but polyphonic pictorial cycle: books first of all, to compose a polychromatic mosaic; stones, fragments of columns left after the bombing; sewing machines; an iron grill; tilted plates of iron; rolls of lead enclosing scraps of coloured materials. From a single opening the stones pour out into the ambulatory like spilt ink. "The theatricality takes shape as the cavity is filled up and becomes a linguistically credible discourse," says Kounellis, like the impenetrable iron plate, closing doors and windows or filling one's mouth with a stone or a toy train, blocks the space and makes it circular, thus avoiding any dispersion. It is like when Piero della Francesca in his *Flagellation* placed a columnar figure in the place reserved for the vanishing point, bringing the depth of the composition to the surface. Windows then acquire further importance. It is through them that light penetrates, light that Kounellis wants to be dramatic and direct, in clear and sharp contrast to shadow, as in Caravaggio's *The Calling of Saint Matthew*. He used lead in 1986 to close all the windows of an abandoned factory in Chicago, allowing light to pass only through small circular cuts. This ideology of shadow, championed by Kounellis as antithetical to the widespread brightness of neon, is expressed by the oil lamp so often found hanging from his sheets of metal; it is the lamp of Van Gogh's *The Potato Eaters*, or wielded by the combatant in Picasso's *Guernica*.

From the shell to the structure was the next step, attacking beams, pillars and buttresses. In 1977, for example, in Tucci Russo's gallery in Turin, Kounellis wrapped a column in a metal spiral with a toy train running around it. In the dialectic between the static nature of the column and the dynamic of the spiral, Kounellis updates the teachings of Francesco Borromini and Frank Lloyd Wright. The same toy train then ran horizontally along a track encircling a column in the cloister of Santa Maria Novella in Florence on the occasion of the *Brunelleschi anticlassico* exhibition in 1978. Presented again in Oxford, this operation performs the antithetical function of cutting the vertical impetus of the column, the same role as performed by the alternating dichromatic bands on the columns of the cathedrals in Orvieto and Siena. In 1991, in Stommeln, the only synagogue to survive the Nazi onslaught in Germany, Kounellis erected three new wooden pillars to prop up the ceiling and the floor of the women's gallery. The dissonant organic element of a stone was embedded between the column and the ceiling like the capital of a Byzantine column. In the multiplicity of later solutions, the load-bearing structure is of wood or iron, while the capitals range from stones to bells, from reams of paper to sheets of iron, from coats to blankets and wardrobes lodged between iron plates and the ceiling.

Finally, two operations on a grand scale: in 1994, invited by the Costopoulos Foundation to present an exhibition in Athens, Kounellis opted for a large cargo vessel used to transport food and anchored in the port of Piraeus, his hometown. If the journey is the metaphor of the artist's trajectory – going, meeting, establishing dialogue and returning – the boat is his favourite means of transport. In 1969, for the poster printed for the exhibition by Lucio Amelio in Naples, Kounellis had himself portrayed in the bow of a fishing boat heading into harbour. In 1993, invited to the Venice Biennial, he hoisted the great many-coloured sails of a fishing boat in the space reserved for him in the Gardens. In the hold of the ship *Ionion*, he occupied every nook and cranny with his history of over thirty years not as a retrospective exhibition but as a one-act play. The second event took place in 1999 in the church of San Augustín in Mexico City, erected in 1692 and second in importance only to the cathedral. Kounellis created a winding pathway in the vast baroque nave marked out by four large square heaps of stone resting on trolleys, the roof hidden by huge white sheets. If these archaic dwellings recalled those frescoed in mediaeval churches, the sheets concealing them picked up on the drapery of the secular statues lining the nave. Encircling the blocks like a crown of thorns was a dance-like array of fallen iron crosses. In the apse, where the original stone crucifix had been dismembered and replaced with a photographic reproduction, Kounellis installed his own double crucifix: a huge T of iron resting on the side windows. Hanging from one of the two arms was the wooden crucifix with a sack of flour pierced by a knife first exhibited in Gubbio in 1996. This duality generated a shattering spatial effect. While the iron cross coincided exactly with the carved one when viewed from the main entrance, the wooden cross avoided any possibility of a perspective fulcrum by virtue of its off-centre location, injecting dynamism into the space and inviting viewers to proceed to the side aisles where a number of the artist's past works, some never before exhibited, rested on iron supports.

The crucifixion, a central theme in the history of Western art, has been a recurrent feature of Kounellis's work since his *Untitled* of 1972, where he placed a pair of small golden shoes at the foot of a wooden cross. In 1997, when Kounellis set off on his still unfinished American tour including Los Angeles, New York, Mexico City, Buenos Aires and Montevideo, he introduced the upside-down version, first as a few specimens made from iron, reiterating them in a dense array like a seismograph. In Bolzano in 2004, he used over fifty iron crosses, coated in red paint, to occupy one of the three bays of a shed where trains are built. They formed a hard and angular horizontal landscape contradicted by a black hat and coat hung in the background; a "humanistic" element *par excellence*, clashing in terms of colour, weight and position. The hat and coat is first encountered in Kounellis's work with *Civil Tragedy* (1975), where it stands out against a gold background, mostly hanging or held between sheets of metal or wrapped around stones and coal. The same forest of crosses was also used in Athens in 2004 to guard a kernel of tables supporting a ring of coal sacks. In Oxford, the crosses occupy one entire room, resting on an expanse of multicoloured kilim rugs. Apart from the contrast between the rigidity of the crosses and the fragility of the humblest of carpets, the work is born, once again "out of a historical situation and establishes itself as indispensable language" in opposition to an unjust war, juxtaposing East and West, industry and handicraft, mass production and unique items embroidered by hand, rigidity and softness, the metallic smell of a factory and the spicy aroma of a souk, monochromatic dullness and polychromatic merriment.

The labyrinth encircling Michelangelo's *Prisoners* in Florence is the latest version of a cycle started in Paris in 2002, continued in Athens and Venice, and reaching its climax in *Atto unico* at the Galleria Nazionale d'Arte Moderna in Rome in 2002. For the first time, the works do not address the space directly but are withdrawn inside a labyrinthine pathway constructed in and against the given environment. In stating that the labyrinth is the opposite of the horses, Kounellis announces a change in course. Simultaneously enclosed and outspread, reassuring and unsettling, Kounellis's labyrinth assumes the dimensions of the environment but is totally detached from it. It coils and expands in a meandering maze, making it necessary to memorize the path in order to find the way out again. Above all, it forbids any totality. The view is always partial, discontinuous, and dynamic; it is the path as well as the search for the path, as in the catacombs. The labyrinth makes it possible to exhibit the past in a way that is not obvious but mysterious, holding fortuitous and unexpected surprises in store: a circle of coal sacks, small scales with coffee, a bed, plaster casts, in short, the memory of other "one-act plays". A diaphragm between work and context, a boundary that defends it and is crossed only by choice, the labyrinth assumes its full significance in relation to the present historical, political and artistic climate.

While Kounellis felt the need in the 1960s to shatter any idea of centrality and open up borders, today he is aware that "this global idea of plurality distances criticism and is a pernicious discourse concealed beneath a libertarian appearance".[24] With its weight, colour and intrusive dust, the heap of coal in a corner, on a shelf, on a table, on top of the labyrinth once again assumes indispensable contemporary relevance in its opposition to the evanescent dispersion of the virtual. This is why, as he concludes in *MicroMega*, "if construction is what counts today, if the virtual era is over, political life could perhaps benefit from the subtle and penetrating skills offered by artists as image builders *par excellence* and people capable of transforming matter, presenting the past on a silver platter, reshaped and, in the most successful cases, resplendant and dialectic." [25]

1
J. Kounellis, 'Il dubbio, l'arte e la passione civile', in *MicroMega* 3/2004, July–August 2004, pp. 172–177

2
The term 'Transavantguardia' was defined by the Italian critic Achille Bonita Oliva in his text 'La Transavanguardia Italiana', published in *Flash Art*, no. 92–93, October-November, 1979

3
S. Luzzatto, *La crisi dell'antifascismo*, Einaudi, Turin 2004

4
Jannis Kounellis, in R. White, 'Interview at Crown Point Press', *View*, Oakland, California, vol.1, n. 10, March 1979. Reprinted in Mario Codognato, Mirta d'Argenzio (eds.) *Echoes in the Darkness. Jannis Kounellis: Writings and Interviews*, Trolley Ltd. London, 2002; pp. 156–177

5
Robert Lumley, 'Spaces of Arte Povera', in R. Flood, F. Morris, (eds.), *Zero to Infinity. Arte Povera 1962–72*, exhibition catalogue, Tate Modern, London, May–August 2001; Minneapolis Walker Art Center, Minneapolis, October 2001–January 2002; Museum of Contemporary Art, Los Angeles, March–August 2002; Hirshhorn Museum and Sculpture Garden, Washington (DC), October 2002–January 2003; pp. 41–62

6
op.cit., p. 62

7
Jannis Kounellis, 'Un uomo antico, un artista moderno', *Odissea Lagunare*, Sellerio Editore, Palermo, 1993, p. 92

8
Jannis Kounellis, 'Interview with Wim Beeren', *Odissea Lagunare*, op.cit., p. 146

9
Jannis Kounellis, 'Interview with Germano Celant', G. Celant (ed.), *Jannis Kounellis*, exhibition catalogue, Musei Communali, Sale d'Arte Contemporanea, Rimini, July-September, 1983; Mazzotta, Milan, 1983, p. 30

10
Micromega, op.cit.

11
Jannis Kounellis in conversation with Bruno Corà, *AEIUO*, n. 1, September 1980, pp. 31–50. Reprinted in *Odissea Lagunare*, op. cit., p. 82

12
Micromega, op.cit.

13
ibid

14
Francesco Bonami, 'Now we begin' in R. Flood, F. Morris, (eds.), op.cit., pp. 109–127

15
ibid, p. 110

16
Germano Celant, 'Arte Povera: Appunti per una guerriglia' in *Flash Art*, no. 5 (November – December, 1967). Reprinted in English in Carolyn Christov-Barkargiev, *Arte Povera*, Phaidon Press Limited, 1999, pp. 194–196

17
'Forward' in I. Giannelli (ed.), *Transavanguardia*, exhibition catalogue, Mostra Castello di Rivoli Museo d'Arte Contemporanea, Rivoli, November 2002 – March 2003, Skira, Milan 2002, pp. 13–14

18
Carolyn Christov-Barkargiev, 'The Italian Avant-Garde: A Re-reading', *Transavanguardia*, op.cit., pp. 69–70

19
G. Celant, 'Non solo pennelli' in *L'Espresso*, 6 February 2003

20
Jannis Kounellis, in Jannis Kounellis, exhibition catalogue, V Premio Pino Pascali, Pinacoteca Provinciale, Bari, March 1979. Reprinted in G. Celant (ed.), Rimini, op. cit, p. 144

21
Achille Bonito Oliva, op.cit.

22
Bruno Corà, op.cit., p81

23
Germano Celant, 'Un'arte povera, un'arte crittica, un'arte iconoclasticta', G. Celant (ed.), *Coerenza incoerenza dall'arte povera al 1984*, exhibition catalogue, Mole Antonelliana, Turin, June–October 1984, Arnoldo Mondadori Editore, Milan 1984, pp. 11–12

24
Micromega, op.cit.

25
ibid

Stain / Macchia

Rudi Fuchs

The black stain on white paper is made with the blackest tar. Such shapes, almost shape-less, have occurred often in the morphology of Jannis Kounellis's work. In many cases they were the agent that, like a flying carpet, carried a scene into being. I remember a long wall (1979) on which an erratic line wandered from left to right, encountering and delimiting various locations for fragments of plaster sculpture placed on small shelves. The sinuous movement of the line, drawn in black chalk, may have recalled a memory of the broad flow of Edvard Munch's brush – but more important is the way the line casually succeeded in unsettling any definition of shape. Imagine following with your eyes the fluttering flight of a butterfly in the summer and then imagine the butterfly describing a line in the air. Similarly, the line on that wall tried to be as unpredictable as the sprightly flight of the butterfly. It is Kounellis's strategy, I know, to delay definitions of form. That is a matter of style; he likes his work to be full of intrigue. Instead of assigning the plaster heads a fixed location, as a classical construction of perspective would do, this wandering line on the white wall was there to unsettle the whole thing. The work then was not at all about these heads; it was about their drifting, as occasioned by the unsettling and mystifying *mise-en-scène*.

Trying to describe this visual plot unfolding before my eyes, another installation came to mind – 1974 in Rome – in which live black birds were hopping and flying about in a room in the gallery. Or further back in time: rooms in which a musician would play on the piano, or the cello or the flute, filling the room with gently flowing sound. Or a slight ballerina dancing before a painting on which is presented the score of the music of her dance. At the time I tended to see these works as little plays, as figurations of some suggestive nar-rative. They were mysterious enough; like the fluttering butterfly that, not for nothing, turns up occasionally in Kounellis's iconography, or the small singing birds, also tiny fluttering things and so nervous in their movement that, unlike the eagle high in the sky, are rarely still. The contour of the eagle does not intrigue Kounellis but the frolicking of the butterfly does.

Pondering those stains of black tar and their strange shapelessness, I began to think that these early works with music were also somehow ambiguous shapes and formulations of shapes in space – invisible, maybe, but certainly imaginable. If we consider the shift-ing positions of letters and their falling out of the distant idea of order that somehow is implicit in their construction, the early letter paintings might also figure in this context. From those early years I also remember drawings, mostly ink and watercolour and some pastel in an informal morphology, in which we see Kounellis creating intuitive shapes with outlines fading like dissolving smoke. And these, in the chronology, were followed by other drawings showing heavy smoke billowing out of tall chimneys, curling upwards and transforming itself into the slender figure of a woman with long hair floating. In other drawings, the curly hair became simply undulating shape. These formal explorations laid the way for larger works such as the famous *Ciminiera* (Chimney) of 1976 and others.

Thus there is a history in Kounellis's work of freely flowing shape and of allowing pliant material to find its own shape: smoke leaving traces of soot, loosely hanging wool or coal poured out of the sack. In most cases, these procedures were part of strategies to formulate and construct more composite works and installations. Over time, the ambiguous shapes appeared less and less. In the last fifteen years or so the works became bigger, heavier and more forbidding. Art had become bigger everywhere; maybe a sense of competition had entered Kounellis's mind. Or, another guess: he felt that the works had to be stark and unsentimental, even gloomy, to establish their authority against the indifferent and modish mundanity of the times. In any case, in Vienna in 1999, the central installation in the exhibition had the violent toughness of a fortification.

The utter blackness of the tar stains is entirely in line with those recent dark works. Otherwise the appearance of the stains (the Italian "macchie" somehow sounds better) is surprising even after the history briefly sketched above – and they make me wonder. The tar comes cold, in cans that are commercially available in the building trade; it has the liquidity of thick syrup. It is poured from the can on the paper and becomes an amount of slush. Kounellis then begins to move the black slush, causing it to spread slowly under its own gravity by nudging it along. For this, he does not use a spatula but, I am told, a small book containing his own writings: a thing close at hand. I imagine him looking intently at the tar spreading gradually into shape. The moving and nudging of the tar sometimes quickens. The brisk movements of the book intervene in the flow and leave wispy traces and occasional spots of tar. In the mass of tar one discerns, here and there, a slight relief – like layered mud that, at low tide, has settled in the bed of the slow river approaching the sea. Then coagulation sets in and the flow stagnates and stops. The stain has reached its shape.

When, some time ago, I first saw these stains on paper I was excited. More than any other aspect it was their tremendous concentration and their magic stillness that intrigued me. I began to compare them to other works on paper I have seen – mostly sketches for installations and thus made with more decisive lines and outlines of shapes. These sketches correspond of course with the strong angularity and physical weight of the actual works as they were completed. Here, with the stains, we see shapes *becoming* shape – slowly moving and spreading. I imagine the artist watching and waiting, as long as it takes, and then wondering where the initial shapelessness would transform itself into an energy of shape. This vision transported me back to those early works with smoke and sound and the fluttering birds and butterflies. I believe that Jannis Kounellis, with these very contemplative stains, may have begun an intimate rephrasing of his work. That happens sometimes with artists when they get older – they go back to the beginning, trying to find the ancient freedom and the old pleasure of flight.

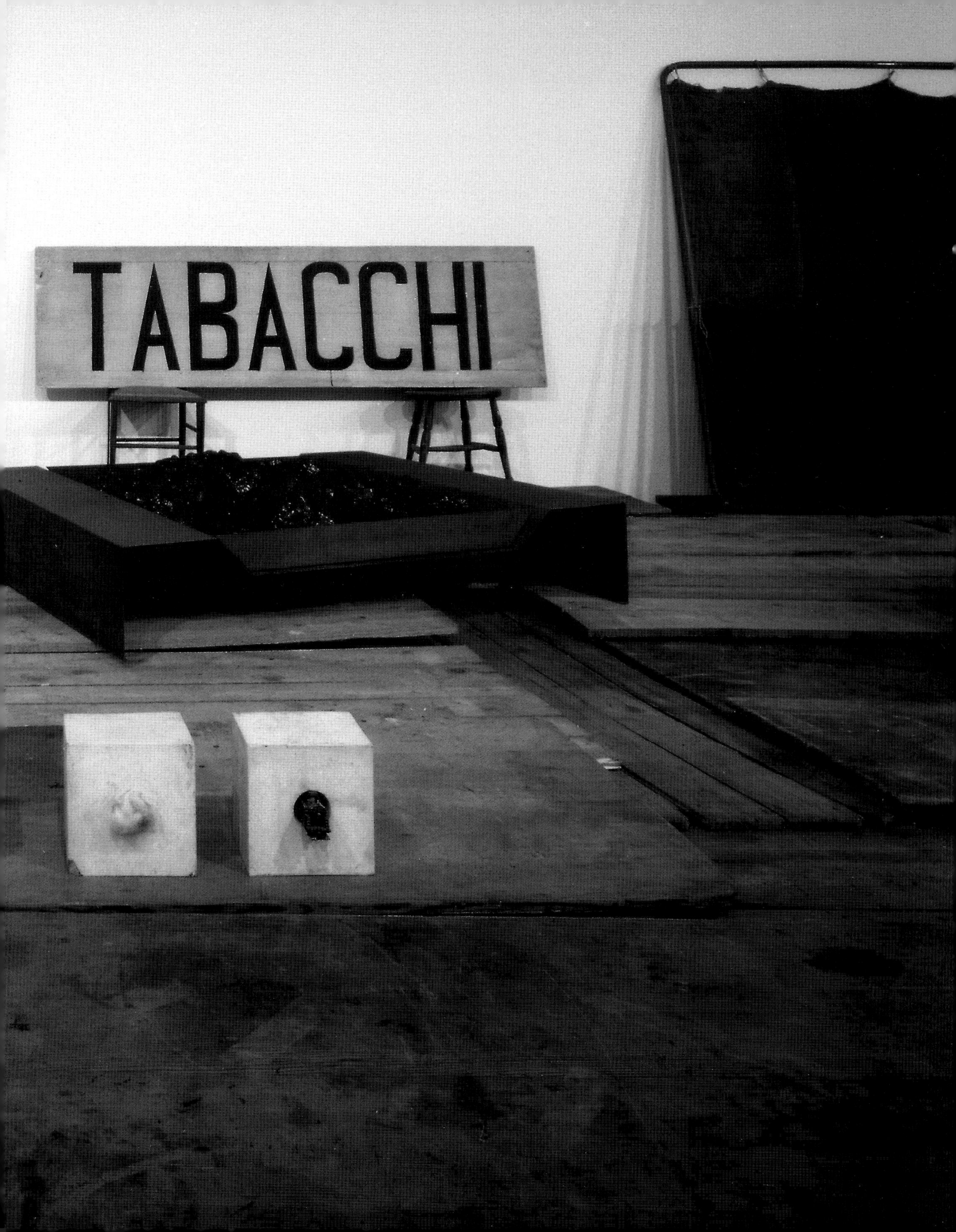
TABACCHI

List of Works

Untitled 1957
Six glass bottles
50 x 10 x 35 cm
Courtesy the artist

Untitled (OLIO/TABACCHI) 1958
Oil on wood
60 x 280 cm
Courtesy the artist

Untitled 1960
Oil on canvas
140 x 230 cm
Courtesy Anthony d'Offay, London

Untitled (Carboniera) 1967
Iron structure, coal
155 x 125 x 30 cm
Courtesy the artist

Untitled (Cotoniera) 1967
Iron structure, cotton
115 x 100 x 100 cm
Raussmüller Collection

Untitled (Margherita di fuoco) 1967
Flower-shaped steel structure
100 (diameter) x 0.15 cm
Collection Mario Pieroni, Rome

Untitled 1967
Aquarium
50 x 25 x 29 cm
Courtesy the artist

Untitled 1967
Three marble cubes, metal toy trains, cotton wool
Each cube: 20 x 20 x 15.5 cm
Courtesy the artist

Untitled 1968
Circle of burlap sacks filled with coal
Dimensions variable
Courtesy the artist

Untitled 1969
Chalk on steel panel, shelf, candle
100 x 70 cm
Reiner Speck Collection, Cologne

Untitled 1969
Steel panel, shelf, egg
100 x 70 cm
Collection Giulio Romieri, Milan

Untitled 1969
Seven burlap sacks filled with red beans, white beans, lentils, rice, coffee beans, corn, potatoes
Dimensions variable
Courtesy the artist

Untitled 1969
Steel bed frame, rolled lead
190 x 90 x 33 cm
Courtesy the artist

Untitled 1969
Hanging steel scales, ground coffee
12 x 12 x 265 cm
Courtesy the artist

Untitled 1969
Coal, white painted line
130 x 120 x 50
Courtesy the artist

Untitled 1969
Burlap sacks sewn together and tied to a steel bed frame
190 x 170 cm
Courtesy the artist

Untitled 1969
Steel shelf, coal
40 x 13 cm
Courtesy the artist

Untitled 1971
Cotton, fly
9 x 9 x 5 cm
Courtesy the artist

Untitled (Florence) 1977
Toy train, motor, steel
Dimensions variable
Courtesy the artist

Untitled 1982
Iron, wood with plaster fragments dipped in black paint
100 x 70 cm
Courtesy the artist

Untitled 1989
Iron plate, iron beam, lead and beetle on cork
100 x 70 x 20 cm
Collection Giuliana and Tommaso Setari

Untitled 1989; Oxford, 2004
Rolled lead
91.4 x 30 (diameter) x 0.9 cm
Courtesy the artist

Untitled 1991
Hard coal pieces and wire on steel panel, seven parts
Each panel: 200 x 180 cm
Galerie Lelong Zurich, Paris

Untitled 1991
Bowl of water with goldfish and knife
35 (diameter) x 13 cm
Courtesy the artist

Untitled 1997
Suspended sewing machine, steel rod
Height variable
Courtesy the artist

Untitled (Mexico City) 1999
Filled canvas bag
Dimensions variable
Courtesy the artist

Untitled (Albatros) 2001
Steel, fragment of a boat, rope of steel
280 x 220 x 60 cm
Courtesy Galerie Kewenig, Cologne

Untitled 2004
Steel plate, paper, tar
200 x 180 x 15 cm
Courtesy the artist

Untitled 2004
Steel plate, paper, tar
200 x 180 x 15 cm
Courtesy the artist

Untitled 2004
Steel plate, paper, tar
200 x 180 x 15 cm
Courtesy the artist

Untitled 2004
Steel crosses, carpets, meat hook, coat, hat
2250 x 700 x 305 cm
Courtesy the artist

Biography

Born in 1936, Piraeus, Greece
Lives and works in Rome, Italy

Solo Exhibitions

1960
Galleria La Tartaruga, Rome (Text, Rome, 1961)

1964
Galleria La Tartaruga, Rome (catalogue)

1966
L'alfabeto, Galleria Arco di Alibert, Rome (catalogue)
Galleria La Tartaruga, Rome (catalogue)

1967
Galleria L'Attico, Rome (catalogue)
Galleria L'Attico, Rome (catalogue)
Kounellis: Il Giardino; I Giuochi, Galleria L'Attico, Rome
(catalogue)

1968
Galleria Iolas, Milan
Galleria Gian Enzo Sperone, Turin

1969
Modern Art Agency, Naples (catalogue: *Bulletin de la
Modern Art Agency, 4*)
Galerie Iolas, Paris
Galleria L'Attico, Rome (catalogue)

1971
Modern Art Agency, Naples
Galleria L'Attico, Rome
Informazione sulla presenza italiana, Incontri Internazionali
d'Arte, Rome (catalogue: *Quaderni del Centro d'Informazione
Alternativa: informazione sulla presenza italiana*, Rome, 1,
1972)
Galleria Gian Enzo Sperone, Turin
Galerie Folker Skulima, Berlin

1972
Sonnabend Gallery, New York

1973
Gallery Iolas, Paris
Galleria La Salita, Rome

1974
Galleria Forma, Genova
Sonnabend Gallery, New York
Galleria Christian Stein, Turin

1975
Galerie Rudolf Zwirner, Cologne
Galleria Lucio Amelio, Naples
Galleria Mario Pieroni, Pescara

1976
Galleria L'Attico, Hotel della Lunetta, Rome
Art in Progress, Düsseldorf (catalogue)
Galleria Salvatore Ala, Milan

1977
Jean & Karen Bernier Gallery, Athens
Kunstmuseum, Lucerne (catalogue)
Villa Pignatelli, Naples
Museum Boymans-van Beuningen, Rotterdam (catalogue)
Studio Tucci Russo, Turin

1978
Galleria Mario Diacono, Bologna (catalogue: *Al di là del circo, nel quadro*)
Städtisches Museum Abteiberg, Mönchengladbach (catalogue)

1979
Jean & Karen Bernier Gallery, Athens (catalogue)
V Premio "Pino Pascali": Jannis Kounellis, Pinacoteca Provinciale, Bari (catalogue)
Galerie Konrad Fischer, Düsseldorf
Museum Folkwang, Essen (catalogue)
Salvatore Ala Gallery, New York
Galleria Christian Stein, Turin

1980
Galerie Konrad Fischer, Düsseldorf
Galleria Lucio Amelio, Naples (catalogue: *Jules Verne: Un capitano di quindici anni – I viaggi straordinari*)
Sonnabend Gallery, New York
ARC/Musée d'Art Moderne de la Ville de Paris, Paris (catalogue)
Galleria Mario Diacono, Rome
Galleria Mario Pieroni, Rome
Galleria Marilena Bonomo, Spoleto
Galerie Annemarie Verna, Zurich

1981
Galerie Karsten Greve, Cologne
Stedelijk Van Abbemuseum, Eindhoven; Obra Social. Caja de Pensiones, Madrid, 1982; Whitechapel Art Gallery, London, 1982; Staatliche Kunsthalle, Baden-Baden, 1982 (catalogue)
Galleria Salvatore Ala, Milan
Galerie Schellmann & Klüser, Munich
Galerie Liliane et Michel Durand-Dessert, Paris

1983
Galerie Konrad Fischer, Düsseldorf
Sonnabend Gallery, New York
Galerie Liliane et Michel Durand-Dessert, Paris

Musei Comunali, Rimini (catalogue)
Galleria Christian Stein, Turin

1984
Museum Haus Esters, Krefeld (catalogue)
Galerie Schellmann & Klüser, Munich
Galleria Lucio Amelio, Naples
Sonnabend Gallery, New York
Galleria Ugo Ferranti, Rome

1985
Jean Bernier Gallery, Athens
capcMusée d'Art Contemporain, Bordeaux (catalogue)
Museum Haus Esters, Krefeld (catalogue)
Galleria Christian Stein, Milan
Städtische Galerie im Lenbachhaus, Munich (catalogue)
Galerie Liliane et Michel Durand-Dessert, Paris

1986
Anthony d'Offay Gallery, London (catalogue)
Galleria Ugo Ferranti, Rome
Galerie Konrad Fischer, Düsseldorf
Jannis Kounellis: A Retrospective, Museum of Contemporary Art, Chicago; Musée d'Art Contemporain, Montreal (catalogue)

1987
Sonnabend Gallery, New York
Galleria Sprovieri, Rome
Artsite Bath Festival, Bath (catalogue)
Institute of Contemporary Art, Nagoya (catalogue)

1988
Galleria Christian Stein, Milan
Galerie Galleria Sparta-Petit, Chagny
Mary Boone Gallery, New York
Castello di Rivoli, Museo d'Arte Contemporanea, Rivoli, Turin, (catalogue)
Galerie Konrad Fischer, Düsseldorf

1989
Donald Young Gallery, Chicago, Illinois
Studio d'Arte Barnabò, Venice
Galerie Lelong, Paris (catalogue)
Espai Poblenou, Barcelona (catalogue)
Ameliobrachot Pièce Unique, Paris (catalogue: *Pièce Unique. "10 anni 1989–1998"*, Milan 1998)
Museo Capodimonte, Naples (catalogue)

1990
Anthony d'Offay Gallery, London
Galleria Opera, Perugia (catalogue: *Opera 1986–1992*, Perugia, 1992)
Margo Leavin Gallery, Los Angeles
Via del Mare, Stedelijk Museum, Amsterdam (catalogue)
La stanza vede, HaagsGemeentemuseum, L'Aia; Arnolfini Gallery, Bristol; ICA, London; Fundaciò Tapiés, Barcelona (catalogue)

1991

The Henry Moore Sculpture Trust Studio at Dean Clough, Halifax (catalogue)
Frammenti di memoria, Kestner-Gesellschaft, Hannover; Kunstmuseum, Winterthur (catalogue)
Casa Centrale degli Artisti, Nuova Tretjakov, Moscow (catalogue)
Galerie Lelong, Zurich (catalogue)
Sinagoga Stommeln, Pulheim (catalogue)

1992

Galleria Lucio Amelio s.r.l., Naples (catalogue)
Galleria Christian Stein, Milan
Padiglione d'Arte Contemporanea, Milan (catalogue)
Mercatello sul Metauro, Urbino (catalogue)

1993

Belvedere, Giardini del Castello, Prague (catalogue)
Real Albergo dei Poveri, Palermo
Kounellis, fumo di pietra, Galerie Lelong, Chatellerault (catalogue: Chatellerault 1994)
Lineare Notturno, Kunsthalle, Recklinghausen (catalogue)
Galerìa Estiarte, Madrid
No and no, but, after all yes, why not, Marian Goodman Gallery, New York (catalogue)

1994

Kounellis, Galerie Lelong, Paris
Cargo Ionion, Piraeus, Athens
Galerie Jean Bernier, Athens
Kounellis, Anthony d'Offay Gallery, London
Galerie Konrad Fischer, Düsseldorf

1995

Galleria d'Arte Moderna "La Salara", Bologna (catalogue)
Chateau de Plieux, Plieux (catalogue)
Galerie Jule Kewenig, Frechen-Bachem
Hamburger Kunsthalle, Hamburg (catalogue)

1996

Galleria Christian Stein, Milan
Jannis Kounellis. La Balera, Galleria Loza Koper, Capodistria (catalogue)
Kounellis. Neue Arbeiten, Galerie Bernd Klüser, Munich (catalogue)
Jannis Kounellis, Castelluccio di Pienza, Siena (catalogue)
Museo Nacional Centro de Arte Reina Sofia, Madrid (catalogue)
Piazza del Plebiscito, Naples (catalogue: *La città in piazza*, 1998)

1997

Rechts-, Sozial- und Wirtschaftswissenschaftliche Fakultat, Karl- Franzens- Universität, Graz
Kounellis. Die Front, das Denken, der Sturm, Museum Ludwig in der Halle Kalk, Cologne (catalogue)

Galleria Gruppo Valtellinese, Refettorio delle Stelline, Milan (catalogue)
Galleria Alfonso Artiaco, Pozzuoli, Naples
Ace Gallery, Los Angeles

1998

Atelier del Bosco di Villa Medici, Rome (catalogue: *Accardi Kounellis Förg Pistoletto Appel*, 1999)
Galleria No Code, Bologna
Jannis Kounellis, Volume!, Rome (catalogue)
Ace Gallery, New York
Galerie Lelong, Paris; Galerie Forsblom, Helsinki 1999; Galeria Carles Taché, Barcelona 1999 (catalogue)
Scultura permanente in via Ponte di Tappia, Naples (catalogue)

1999

Galerie Karsten Greve, Cologne
Jannis Kounellis. Il Sarcofago degli Sposi, Museum für angewandte Kunst, Vienna (catalogue)
Jannis Kounellis, Chiesa di San Augustin, – UNAM, Mexico City (catalogue: *Jannis Kounellis en Mexico*, 2000)

2000

Jannis Kounellis. Ein Saal für die Sammlung, Kunstmuseum Winterthur, Winterthur
Castello Colonna, Genazzano
Jannis Kounellis, Museo Nacional de Belas Artes, Buenos Aires
Jannis Kounellis, Reti, via S. Nicola de' Cesarini, Rome
Galleria Christian Stein, Milan

2001

Jannis Kounellis. Bilder 1958–1968. Objekte 1968–2000, Galerie Karsten Greve, Cologne
Jannis Kounellis, Museo Nacional de Artes Visuales, Montevideo
Kounellis, Centro per l'Arte Contemporanea Luigi Pecci, Prato (catalogue)
Kounellis, Bottini dell'Olio, Livorno (catalogue)
Jannis Kounellis. Albatros & The Gospel According to Thomas, Galerie Jule Kevenig, Frechen-Bachem
Jannis Kounellis, Kunst-Station Sankt Peter, Cologne; Diözesanmuseum Freising, Freising, 2001–2002 (catalogue)

2002

Kounellis, Galerie Lelong, Paris; Galerie Forsblom, Helsinki, 2002; Galeria Carles Taché, Barcelona, 2003 (catalogue)
Inaugurazione della stazione della metropolitana di piazza Dante, Naples
Jannis Kounellis: Senza Titolo…, Hallen für neue Kunst, Schaffhausen
Kounellis, Stedelijk Museum voor Aktuele Kunst, Gand (catalogue)
Jannis Kounellis. Atto Unico, Galleria Nazionale d'Arte Moderna, Rome (catalogue)

2003

Jannis kounellis. Installation, Galleri Bo Bjerggaard, Copenhagen (catalogue)
Jannis Kounellis i Sct. Johannes Kirke, Sct. Johannes Kirke, Herning (catalogue)
Kounellis, Galleria Christian Stein, Milan
Jannis Kounellis, Torrione Passari, Molfetta (catalogue)
Jannis Kounellis, Monastero Mechitarista, Isola di San Lazzaro degli Armeni, Venice (catalogue)
Aula del Palazzo dell'Unesco, Paris
Jannis Kounellis, Kunstraum Innsbruck, Innsbruck (catalogue)
Jannis Kounellis, Galleria Fumagalli, Bergamo

2004

Jannis Kounellis. New Works, Sprovieri, London
Terre di confine. Con-fine dell'Arte, Palazzo Lantieri, Gorizia
Kounellis in Sarajevo, Vijecnica/National Library, Sarajevo (catalogue)
Jannis Kounellis, Megaron – The Athens Concert Hall, Athens (catalogue)
Kounellis, Galerie Karsten Greve, Cologne
Jannis Kounellis, Modern Art Oxford, Oxford (catalogue)

Selected Group Exhibitions

1961

Kounellis, Rauschenberg, Schifano, Tinguely, Twombly, Galleria La Tartaruga, Rome

1963

13 pittori a Roma, Galleria La Tartaruga, Rome (catalogue)

1967

Arte povera e IM spazio, Galleria La Bertesca, Genova (catalogue)
V Biennale de Paris, ARC/Musée d'art moderne de la ville de Paris, Paris, (catalogue)
Lo spazio degli elementi: Fuoco immagine acqua terra, Galleria l'Attico, Rome (catalogue)
11 artisti italiani degli anni '60, Palazzo Ancaiani, Spoleto (catalogue)

1968

Arte povera+azioni povere, Arsenali dell'Antica Repubblica, Amalfi (catalogue)
Young Italians, Institute of Contemporary Art, Boston; Jewish Museum, New York (catalogue)
Fabro, Kounellis, Paolini, Galleria Qui Arte Contemporanea, Rome (catalogue)

1969

Op Losse Schroeven, Stedelijk Museum, Amsterdam (catalogue)
When Attitudes Become Form, Kunsthalle, Berne; Museum Haus Lange, Krefeld; Institute of Contemporary Arts, London (catalogue)
Prospect 69, Städtische Kunsthalle, Düsseldorf
I materiali, Galleria Qui Arte Contemporanea, Rome (catalogue)

1970

Amore Mio, Palazzo Ricci, Montepulciano (catalogue)
Fine dell'alchimia – De Dominicis, Kounellis, Pisani, Galleria L'Attico, Rome (catalogue)
Vitalità del negativo nell'arte italiano 1960–1970, Palazzo delle Esposizioni, Rome (catalogue)
Between Man and Matter: Tokio Biennale '70, Metropolitan Art Gallery, Tokyo (catalogue)
Conceptual Art, Arte Povera, Land Art, Galleria Civica d'Arte Moderna, Turin (catalogue)

1971

International Theatre Festival: Persona, Belgrade, Zagreb (catalogue)
Arte Povera, 13 Italian Artists, Kunstverein Munich (catalogue)
VII Biennale de Paris, Bois de Vincennes, Paris (catalogue)

1972

Documenta 5, Kassel (catalogue)
XXXV Biennale, Venice (catalogue: *XXXV Biennale di Venice: Persona 2*)

1973

An Exhibition of New Italian Art, The Arts Council of Northern Ireland Gallery, Belfast (catalogue)
Italy two: Art around '70, Museum of the Philadelphia Civic Center, Philadelphia (catalogue)
Contemporanea, Parcheggio di Villa Borghese, Rome (catalogue)

1974

Arman, Cane, Christo, Kienholz, Kounellis, Tacchi, Musée d'Art Moderne, Strasbourg (catalogue)
XXXVI Biennale, Venice (catalogue)

1975

Eight Artists, Eight Attitudes, Eight Greeks, Institute of Contemporary Arts, London (catalogue)

1976

Prospect Retrospect: Europa 1946–1976, Städtische Kunsthalle, Düsseldorf (catalogue)
XXXVII Biennale, Venice (catalogue: *XXXVII Biennale di Venice: Ambiente/Arte: Dal Futurismo alla body art*, Venice, 1977)

1977

Omaggio a Brunelleschi, Chiostro di Santa Maria Novella, Florence
Beuys, Kounellis, Lee Byars, Sperone Westwater Fischer, New York
Joseph Beuys, Jannis Kounellis, Mario Merz, Marisa Merz, Festival of Celtic People, Wrexham, UK
Documenta 6, Kassel (catalogue)

1978

XXXVIII Biennale, Venice (catalogue: *XXXVIII Biennale di Venice: Artenatura*)
A.R. Penck, Robert Ryman, Sol LeWitt, Jannis Kounellis, InK. Halle für internationale neue Kunst, Zurich (catalogue: InK. *Dokumentation 1*)

1979

Gino De Dominicis, Jannis Kounellis, Ettore Spalletti, Galleria Mario Pieroni, Rome

1980

100 years of Italian Modern Art 1880–1980, Italian Cultural Institute, Tokyo (catalogue)
Kunst in Europa na '68, Museum Van Hedendaagse Kunst, Citadelpark en Centrum voor Kunst en Cultuur St. Pietersplein, Gent (catalogue)

1981

A New Spirit in Painting, The Royal Academy of Arts, London (catalogue)
Che fare? Kounellis, Merz, Nauman, Serra, Museum Haus Lange, Krefeld (catalogue)
Baselitz, Kounellis, Paolini, Penk, Galleria Christian Stein, Turin
Identité italienne. L'art en Italie depuis 1959, Musée National d'Art Moderne, C.N.A.C. Georges Pompidou, Paris (catalogue)

1982

Arte Povera, Antiform, Centre d'Arts Plastiques Contemporains, Bordeaux (catalogue)
"The Italians". From arte povera to transavanguardia, Marianne Deson Gallery, Chicago
Kiefer, Kounellis, Merz, Galleria Christian Stein, Turin
Kunst wird Material, Nationalgalerie, Berlin (catalogue)
Zeitgeist, Martin Gropius-Bau, Berlin (catalogue)
Documenta 7, Kassel (catalogue)
Arte Italiana, Institute of Contemporary Arts and Hayward Gallery, London (catalogue)
Spelt from Sibyl's Leaves. Explorations in Italian Art, Power Gallery, University of Sydney; University Art Museum, University of Queensland, Brisbane, Australia (catalogue)

1983

Anselmo, Kounellis, Merz, Galleria Christian Stein, Turin
ARS 83, The Art Museum of Athensum, Helsinki (catalogue)
The Sculpture Show, Hayward Gallery and Serpentine Gallery, London (catalogue)

1984

Carl Andre, Joseph Beuys, Donald Judd, Jannis Kounellis, Sol LeWitt, Richard Long, Robert Mangold, Mario Merz, Bruce Nauman, Robert Ryman and Lawrence Weiner, Hallen für neue Kunst, Schaffhausen (catalogue)
Légendes, capcMusée d'art contemporain, Bordeaux (catalogue)
XLI Biennale, Venice (catalogue)
Coerenza in Coerenza: dall'Arte Povera al 1984, Mole Antonelliana, Turin (catalogue)
Kounellis, Paolini, Buren, Weiner, Kirkeby, daadgalerie, Berlin
Ouverture, Castello di Rivoli, Museo d'Arte Contemporanea, Rivoli, Turin (catalogue)

1985

Del arte Povera a 1985, Palacio Valàzquez, Palacio de Cristal, Madrid (catalogue)
The European Iceberg, Art Gallery of Ontario, Toronto (catalogue)
Don Giovanni, Stedelijk Van Abbemuseum, Eindhoven
The Knot: Arte Povera at P.S.1, P.S.1, The Institute for Art and Urban Resources, New York (catalogue)
1985 Carnegie International, Museum of Art, Carnegie Institute, Pittsburgh (catalogue)
The Iron Window, Stedelijk Van Abbemuseum, Eindhoven (catalogue)

1986

Joseph Beuys, Enzo Cucchi, Anselm Kiefer, Jannis Kounellis, Kunsthalle, Basel (catalogue)
Falls the Shadow: Recent British and European Art, Hayward Gallery, London (catalogue)
Jannis Kounellis, Sol Lewitt, Richard Long, Bruce Nauman, Martin Puryear, Ulrich Wien Fluss, Wiener Secession and Am Steinhof, Vienna (catalogue)
Chambre d'amis, Museum Van Hedendaagse Kunst, Gand (catalogue)
Rückriem. Installations and Sculpture, Donald Young Gallery, Chicago
Sol LeWitt, Jannis Kounellis, Galleria Mario Pieroni, Rome

1987

L'époque, la mode, la morale, la passion, Musée National d'Art Moderne, C.N.A.C. Georges Pompidou, Paris (catalogue)
From the Europe of old, Stedelijk Museum, Amsterdam (catalogue)

1988

Kounellis, Serra, Tapies, Jean and Karen Bernier Gallery, Athens
XLIII Biennale, Venice (catalogue)
Baselitz, Kounellis, Twombly, Galleria Lucio Amelio, Naples
1988, Carnegie International, The Carnegie Museum of Art, Pittsburgh (catalogue)

1989

Italian Art in the Twentieth Century, The Royal Academy of Arts, London (catalogue)
Verso l'Arte Povera, Padiglione d'Arte Contemporanea, Milan (catalogue)

1990

Jannis Kounellis, Bruce Nauman, Ulrich Rückriem, Richard Serra, Antoni Tapies, Donald Young Gallery, Chicago (catalogue)
Affinities and Intuitions, The Art Institute of Chicago, Chicago
Die Endlichkeit der Freiheit, Berlin 1990 – Ein Ausstellungsprojekt in Ost und West, Berlin (catalogue)
Memoria del futuro, Museo Nacional Reina Sofia, Madrid

1991

Metropolis, Martin Gropius-Bau, Berlin (catalogue)

1992

Allegories of Modernism: contemporary drawing, The Museum of Modern Art, New York (catalogue)
Platzverführung, Schwäbisch Gmünd (catalogue)
Configuracions urbanes, Barcelona (catalogue: *Urban Configurations*, 1994)

1993

Gravity and Grace, Hayward Gallery, London (catalogue)
David Hammons, Jannis Kounellis, American Academy, Rome (catalogue)
XLV Biennale, Venice (catalogue)

1994

The Tradition af the New: Postwar Masterpieces from the Guggenheim Collection, Solomon Guggenheim Museum, New York
The Italian Metamorphosis, 1943–1968, Solomon Guggenheim Museum, New York
Giovanni Anselmo, Jannis Kounellis, Juan Munoz, Thomas Schütte, Galerie Jean Bernier, Athens
Lavori Nuovi, Domenico Bianchi, Christian Boltanski, Jannis Kounellis, Galleria Ugo Ferranti, Rome

1995

Wild at Heart, Tramway, Glasgow
Where is Abel thy brother?, Galleria Nazionale d'Arte Moderna Zacheta, Warsaw (catalogue)

Duck Not On A Pond, Ganders Never Laid A Golden Egg, Rochdale Canal, Central Manchester
Main Stations, Casino Luxembourg, Luxembourg (catalogue)
4th International Istanbul Biennial, St. Irene, Istanbul (catalogue)

1996

Portrait of the artist, Anthony d'Offay Gallery, London
Ars Aevi 2000, Centro per l'Arte Contemporanea Luigi Pecci, Prato (catalogue)
Rebecca Horn Jannis Kounellis, Galerie Franck & Schülte, Berlin (catalogue

1997

For Heiner Müller, Centro de Exposicoes, Galeria das Caravelas, Centro Cultural de Belem, Lisbon (catalogue)
Città Natura, Mercati di Traiano, Palazzo delle Esposizioni e altre sedi, Rome (catalogue)
Modern Art in the 20th Century, Martin Gropius-Bau, Berlin (catalogue)
De Re Metallica, Anthony d'Offay Gallery, London
Donald Judd, Jannis Kounellis, Arnulf Rainer, Stedelijk Museum, Amsterdam
Arte Italiana 1945–1995. Il visibile e l'invisibile, Aichi Prefectural Museum of Art, Nagoya; Museum of Contemporary Art, Tokyo; Yonago City Museum of Art, Tottori; Hiroshima City Museum of Contemporary Art, Hiroshima, 1998

1998

Out of Actions: Between Performance and the Object, 1949–1979, The Geffen Contemporary at Museum of Contemporary Art, Los Angeles; MAK, Museum für ange-wandte Kunst, Vienna, 1998; Museu d'Art Contemporani, Barcelona, 1998–1999; Museum of Contemporary Art, Tokyo, 1999 (catalogue)
Wounds: Between democracy and redemption in contemporary art, Moderna Museet, Stockholm (catalogue)
artranspennine98, Henry Moore Studio at Dean Clough, Halifax and other sites in Liverpool, Manchester, Leeds, Hull (catalogue)

1999

Examining Pictures: Exhibiting paintings, Whitechapel Art Gallery, London; Museum of Contemporary Art, Chicago (catalogue)
Regarding Beauty. A View of the Late Twentieth Century, Hirshhorn Museum and Sculpture Garden, Washington; Haus der Kunst, Munich, 2000

2000

Lavori al Castello Doria-Pamphili, Valmontone
A Tribute to Robert Hopper, Yorkshire Sculpture Park, West Bretton, Wakefield (England)
Anima, Monastero delle Lucrezie, Todi (catalogue)
Giganti, Arte Contemporanea nei Fori Imperiali, Scavi dei Fori Imperiali, Rome

Il Parco di scultura di Villa Glori, Parco di Villa Glori, Rome (catalogue)
Anselmo, Merz, Penone, Kounellis, Laib, Galerie Konrad Fischer, Düsseldorf
Novecento, Arte e Storia in Italia, Scuderie Papali del Quirinale, Mercati di Traiano, Rome (catalogue)

2001
1 Gennaio 2001, Emilio, Luigi Ontani, Jannis Kounellis, Franz West, Zerynthia, Rome (catalogue)
Bianchi, Kounellis, Paladino, Galleria No Code, Bologna
Zero to Infinity: Arte Povera 1962–1972, Tate Modern, London; Walker Art Center, Minneapolis, 2001–2002; The Museum of Contemporary Art, Los Angeles, 2002; Hirshhorn Museum and Sculpture Garden, Washington, D.C., 2002 (catalogue)
Jannis Kounellis, Giorgio Morandi, Sprovieri, London (catalogue)

2002
A Short History of Performance: Part One, Whitechapel Art Gallery, London
Contrappunto, Rebecca Horn, Jannis Kounellis, Galleria La Nuova Pesa, Rome
Les années 70: l'art en cause, capcMusée d'art contemporain, Bordeaux
Arteinmemoria, Scavi di Ostia, Centrale Montemartini, Ostia e Rome (catalogue)
Incontri, Galleria Borghese, Rome (catalogue)

2003
Una piazza per Leonardo, Cinque progetti per il nuovo ingresso del museo leonardiano, Museo Leonardiano, Palazzina Uzielli, Vinci (catalogue)
Grazie, Historie Landschaft, Schloss Dyck, Jüchen (catalogue)
Outlook, Technopolis, Athens (catalogue)

2004
Intra-muros, Musée d'Art Moderne et d'Art Contemporain, Nice (catalogue)

Selected Reading

Books

Stephen Bann, *Jannis Kounellis*, Reaktion Books Ltd. London, 2003

Carolyn Christov-Bakargiev, *Arte Povera*, Phaidon, 1999

Mario Codognato and Mirta D'Argenzio (eds.), *Echoes in the Darkness: Writings and Interviews 1966– 2002*, Trolley, 2002

Catalogues

Jannis Kounellis, Stedelijk Van Abbemuseum, Eindhoven, 1981; Obra Social, Caixa de Pensions, Madrid, 1982; Whitechapel Art Gallery, London, 1982 and Staatliche Kunsthalle, Baden-Baden, 1982; Text by Rudi Fuchs

Jannis Kounellis, Anthony d'Offay, London, 1986; Text by Lynn Cooke

Jannis Kounellis: A Retrospective, Museum of Contemporary Art, Chicago, 1986; Text by Thomas McEvilley

Jannis Kounellis, Artsite Gallery, Bath International Festival, 1987; Text by Mark Francis

The Henry Moore Sculpture Trust Studio at Dean Clough, Halifax, 1993; Texts by Barry Barker and Sir Alan Bowness

David Hammons, Jannis Kounellis, American Academy in Rome, 1993; Text by Robert Storr

Zero to Infinity: Arte Povera 1962–1972, Cantz Verlag, Germany and Tate Gallery Publishing Limited, London, 2001; Texts by Francesco Bonami, Giorgia Bottinelli, Carolyn Christov-Bakargiev, Corinna Criticos, Richard Flood, Robert Lumley, Frances Morris and Karen Pinkus

Jannis Kounellis Giorgio Morandi, Sprovieri, London, 2001; Text by Achille Bonito Oliva

Jannis Kounellis

Modern Art Oxford
15 December 2004 – 20 March 2005

Organised by Modern Art Oxford

Curators: Suzanne Cotter and Andrew Nairne
Assistant Curator: Miria Swain
Programme Administrator: Dawn Scarfe
Gallery Manager: Tom Legg
Head of Marketing and Development: Kirsty Brackenridge
Press and Marketing Officer: Rachel Tomkins
Communications Administrator: Meera Hindocha

Jannis Kounellis has been made possible by a generous bequest from the Estate of the Late Tom Bendhem, a Patron of the Gallery. Also supported by The Henry Moore Foundation, The Italian Cultural Institute and The Stanley Thomas Johnson Foundation.

Thanks to Pegasus Engineering

With special thanks to those Patrons and Friends who have individually supported the exhibition:

Patrons:
John Barrow, Sir Patrick Nairne, Eve and Godfrey Pilkington, Marion and Robert Rickman, Jill Ritblat, Charlotte and Dennis Stevenson, Robert and Felicity Waley-Cohen.

Friends:
Madeleine Bessborough, Sir Alan Bowness, Colin Bradley, Helen and Sebastian Brock, Julie Carter, Margaret Curtis, Dr Roy Darke and Dr Jane Darke, R. De Felice, Amanda de G. Morrison, Steve and Frances Fairman, Jean Flemming, Sissel Fowler, Sarah Galloway, Jane Garnett, Dr Martin I. Gaughan, Betty and Morton Hooper, John and Pauline Hunter, Sir Rex Richards, Mark P. Robbins, Jeanne Wesson

and those Patrons and Friends who wish to remain anonymous

With thanks to Joel Anitori, Mirta d'Argenzio, Ermanno Arslan, Manolis Baboussis, Sylvia Bandi, Stefania Bonelli, Vangjel Caci, Elisabetta Compolongo, Michelle Coudray, Mario Codognato, Mauro De Rossi, Emma Digerud-Waring, Anthony d'Offay, James Elliot, Douglas Fisher, Dr Mario Fortunato, Jean Frémon, Rudi Fuchs, Inès Goldbach, Monika Görlich, David Head, David Isaac, Michael Kewenig, Herman Lelie, Vita Moltedo, Urs Rausmüller, Laura Ricketts, Joseph Schnyder, Nicholas Serota, Giuliana and Tommaso Setari, Reiner Speck, Nicholas Sprovieri and Sprovieri Gallery, London, Anne Steinberg, Stuart Turner, Damiano Urbani, Anne Unthank, Cliff Vernon, Martin Wilkinson, Ben Young, Adachiara Zevi

Italian Cultural Institute

STANLEY THOMAS JOHNSON FOUNDATION

The Henry Moore Foundation

We extend our thanks to Illycaffé who have generously supported this publication

Published by Modern Art Oxford
Edited by Suzanne Cotter assisted by Miria Swain
The Visual Poetics of Jannis Kounellis: Suzanne Cotter and Andrew Nairne
An Engaged Modern Painter: Adachiara Zevi
Translation: Paul T. Metcalfe
Stain/Macchia: Rudi Fuchs
Installation photography: Manolis Baboussis.
All other images: Claudio Abate
Designed by Herman Lelie
Typeset by Stefania Bonelli
Printed by Dexter, UK in an edition of 1500 copies

ISBN: 1 901 352 23 4
Distributed in the UK by Cornerhouse
70 Oxford Street, Manchester M1 5NH, England
Tel: + 44 (0)161 200 1503
Fax: + 44 (0)161 200 1504
email: publications@cornerhouse.org
www.cornerhouse.org/publications

Modern Art Oxford
30 Pembroke Street
Oxford OX1 1BP
England
Tel: + 44 (0) 1865 722 733
Fax: + 44 (0) 1865 722 573
www.modernartoxford.org.uk

Modern Art Oxford is supported by Oxford City Council, Arts Council England, South East, and the Horace W. Goldsmith Foundation.
Museum of Modern Art. Registered charity no. 313035

supported by